THE UNIVERSE AND I WALKED INTO A BAR

How all of existence is one and other stuff

Dearest Samantha,

Thank you for coming into my life.
I love you with all of the universe within us.

Copyright 2019 © by Kai Teo All Rights Reserved

No part of this book may be reproduced or transmitted in any form by any means: graphic, electronic, or mechanical, including photocopying, recording, taping or by any information storage or retrieval system without permission, in writing, from the authors, except for the inclusion of brief quotations in a review, article, book, or academic paper. The authors and publisher of this book and the associated materials have used their best efforts in preparing this material. The authors and publisher make no representations or warranties with respect to accuracy, applicability, fitness or completeness of the contents of this material. They disclaim any warranties expressed or implied, merchantability, or fitness for any particular purpose. The authors and publisher shall in no event be held liable for any loss or other damages, including but not limited to special, incidental, consequential, or other damages. If you have any questions or concerns, the advice of a competent professional should be sought.

Disclaimer: This book is non-fiction. All names, identities, and/or personal characteristics of any individual involved have been changed to protect and disguise their identities. So, if you read something somewhere that resembles someone living or dead, that is pure coincidence and unintentional.

Acknowledgements

This book would not have been possible without the amazing work of Olivia, Eyal, and the beautiful sacred medicine Yopo.

I would also like to give my most heartfelt gratitude to the crowdfunders who have shown me unwavering support and patience throughout the creation of this book.

Loads of love to:

- Global Tribe Biodynamic Ecovillage, for always giving me a home to feel free in
- Warriors Path - KrigerensVej.dk
- Stefan Brunschwiler
- Carsten Gundel
- Karoline Maréchaux
- Thomas Pedersen, Mankind Clothing
- Kristina Rove
- Cecilia Karlsson
- Stéphane Gerber

CONTENTS

Introduction — 6
Open your doors of perception, it's happy hour

Chapter 1 — 11
Set and setting

Chapter 2 — 17
The shaman

Chapter 3 — 22
The ceremony

Chapter 4 — 28
The medicine

Chapter 5 — 33
The blueprint of the Universe

Chapter 6 — 38
Why are you speaking in my voice?

Chapter 7 — 42
You're fine

Chapter 8 — 45
Why do we exist?

Chapter 9 — 50
Is the Universe love?

Chapter 10 — 54
Why do we desire enlightenment?

Chapter 11 Do you believe in karma?	59
Chapter 12 Did the religions get it right?	65
Chapter 13 The emptiness and fullness of the ego	70
Chapter 14 So everything is perfect? Including Trump?	74
Chapter 15 Is there hope for humanity? Are we waking up?	80
Chapter 16 What about the new age stuff?	85
Chapter 17 The shaman doesn't read horoscopes	91
Chapter 18 The highest form of spirituality	95
Chapter 19 Manifesting stuff	100
Chapter 20 Waking up to a life of service	104

- INTRODUCTION -

OPEN YOUR DOORS OF PERCEPTION, IT'S HAPPY HOUR!

Introduction - Open your doors of perception, it's happy hour!

It must have been over a decade ago when I first embarked on the journey to explore my consciousness. Yes, it was psychedelics that opened the doors to my own deeper existence, it was LSD and psilocybin mushrooms that helped give me a clearer insight into life, and thanks to these medicines, I'm able to sit here today to begin writing this book, to share with you everything that I've learnt.

Not like I know better about anything than you do, I've just been lucky enough to be able to pluck out some little fruits of wisdom from our eternal, combined consciousness. And today, I would like to share them with you – no self righteousness, no "holier than thou join my sex cult I am your guru" bullshit. Kinda like I bought a watermelon and I'm offering you a slice, not gonna judge you for not having money to buy a watermelon, nor be all proud and shit because I am more generous than you. Just sharing, freely.

I understand that many of my friends and other spiritual seekers do not condone the use of substances in the path of reaching a higher self. I fully respect your personal journey and also see the possibility of attaining spiritual fulfilment through meditation and other practices.

However, I also seek your kind understanding in the entheogenic paths of ancient sages, medicine men and women, and energy healers. They have been practicing their arts and

Introduction - Open your doors of perception, it's happy hour!

sciences for thousands and thousands of years, and evidence of their contribution to the welfare and preservation of the planet and its inhabitants is undeniable.

I sincerely hope you will read this book with an open heart, and not judge me for sharing my watermelon, just because you're more of a grapefruit kind of person.

Over the past years, I'm deeply grateful that my own learning from entheogenic medicines – psychoactive substances used for the purpose of self discovery, spiritual exploration, and learning – has indeed made me a kinder, less materialistic, more compassionate human being. But it's like going out for happy hour, once you drink the first pint from the universal brewery of knowledge, you want the next pint, and the next, and by the end of the evening, you're doing tequila shots and downing some weird rainbow coloured flaming drink.

With psychedelic exploration, once we see that there's something more than this 9 to 5, get married, have children, die of cancer kinda life, we're often too eager to find out what's more. I've seen the plants breathe and the oceans sing, but what is their message? I've felt myself becoming one with the planet, but why are we One? Who is The One? The current systems of modern life are fucked up, but isn't it all going according to the universe's plan?

Introduction - Open your doors of perception, it's happy hour!

In order to pursue the answers to our endless questions, we often think, "Maybe one more tab of acid would open my mind up even more, maybe even 1200 micrograms", or "How about DMT? We push into the breakthrough, meet the entities, come back, then re-enter", or even, "Maybe one more Ayahuasca session with the shaman and I'll be satisfied, if not, I'll come back again next summer."

I too, have pushed myself to the limits of my own sanity, often venturing into the realms of what has been mistakenly termed "heroic doses". You know, just to see what's more, to see what the human mind is capable of; to see if I really am a hero. Every time, I've come back learning that there really is nothing heroic about my ability to take psychedelic punches, I mean, what was I trying to prove? But of course, the thirst for knowledge, and the ego's thirst for its own gratification, was a difficult to satisfy one.

After every trip, I return with tons of souvenirs, numerous glimpses of wisdom, and more answers than I asked for. But there was always one more question that I wanted to ask, one more "truth" that I was seeking. Am I not smart enough? Am I not worthy of the whole truth? Which substance can give me the ultimate trip and give me the full apple from the Tree of Knowledge? Next time we'll take more, psychedelic hero. Maybe then, we'll see.

Introduction - Open your doors of perception, it's happy hour!

I chased, and I chased hard. Maybe because I thought I could gain enlightenment this way, or maybe because I could somehow, casually mention in the next conversation about the time I went for 1000 micrograms on the festival dance floor, get looks of approval or even the occasional "You're crazy". And then, I'd somehow deny that I was actually proud of it and boasting to you, but instead, trying to give you advice because I'm "wiser" than you. "I've experienced ego-loss more times that you, so here's what I have to say."

Spiritual teachers, friends, respectable musicians and artists – everyone's going on and on about Ayahuasca, natural medicines, and life-changing ceremonies. Naturally, I wanted to move my exploration further into the realms of the gods, venture beyond the festival grounds, and soak in the precious nectar of knowledge the ancient shamans have known for thousands of years. I wasn't really into meeting entities, or go on a deep trip about the regrets and pain in my life. I wanted the holy grail, I wanted to meet the Universe itself.

So here's how it all began, the grand rollercoaster ride that ended my pursuit, the one trip that stopped me from chasing further, and the big boom boom that told me that there was nothing more to discover. Come with me, happy hour has just begun.

– CHAPTER 1 –
SET AND SETTING

Chapter 1 – Set and setting

I looked out the window and the empty streets were covered with fresh, white snow. Life seemed to have taken a pause as the dim twilight bathed the city in a melancholic grey-blue filter. Everything was still, except for the occasional car, with headlights projecting two clear beams into the fog, driving slowly past the apartment building. And every once in a while, I'll see someone fully wrapped up in a thick winter jacket and giant scarf striding past briskly on their way somewhere.

It was February in Malmö, Sweden. Many would call these winter months depressing, but for me, there's always been a comforting vibe to the whole Scandinavia darkness, especially when we've got candles lit, a coffee brewing, and someone cooking in the kitchen.

I was home with Olga, one of my best friends, whom I have been living with for the past few months. Normally, we would be binging on Netflix episodes and eating all kinds of junk. But today was different. We were expecting someone, some experience, some transition. In the silence of winter, my body was tingling with anticipation.

Today was going to be the day of our Yopo ceremony. Olga had decided to host the shaman, whom she had known for years, to come to us to deliver an out-of-this-world experience to our consciousness, so that we could learn and grow from it.

Chapter 1 - Set and setting

Yopo, also known as *Anadenanthera peregrina* in Latin, is a tree native to South America and the Caribbean. Its seeds are known to contain the hallucinogen DMT, or N-Dimethyltryptamine, the strongest psychedelic known to humankind. DMT is also the active ingredient in *Ayahuasca*, a more well-known plant that is now being used in self-discovery journeys all across the planet.

Even though it has not become part of popular spiritual culture, Yopo has been used in rituals and ceremonies in South America for thousands of years. The oldest clear evidence of its use came from the Inca Cueva, a site in Jujuy Province, Argentina. Pipes made from puma bones were found alongside Yopo seeds by archaeologists and radiocarbon dating showed that the pipes were from 2130 BC, suggesting that Yopo has been used as a hallucinogen for over 4000 years.[1] So yea, this form of spirituality is more ancient than most religions.

Yopo seeds are traditionally grounded into a powder and inhaled through the nose either by the user or blown into the nostrils by the shaman. To further enhance the entheogenic (substance taken for spiritual or self discovery) effects of the

---

[1] Pochettino, M. L.; Cortella, A. R.; Ruiz, M. (1999). "Hallucinogenic Snuff from Northwestern Argentina: Microscopical Identification of Anadenanthera colubrina var. cebil (Fabaceae) in Powdered Archaeological Material". *Economic Botany.* **53** (2): 127-132.

13

Chapter 1 – Set and setting

seed, many tribes would also chew the *caapi* herb before or while taking Yopo so that the DMT would break down slower in the body, thus creating a longer lasting reaction. In natural rainforests, these two plants usually grow more than 50 kilometres apart from each other, so it took a profound knowledge of all the forest herbs to understand that these two substances could work together – a deep wisdom humanity should learn to preserve and respect.

I had never taken such a strong hallucinogen before. Yes, I've smoke DMT a few times, but the trip was over in a matter of minutes, and it had always been at some festival, on a dance floor, where I had never really allowed myself to explore its full effects, or shown it the kind of respect it as I would in a proper ceremony.

Naturally, I was a little nervous. But I knew that my psychedelic exploration through LSD and mushrooms has somehow reached a plateau, and I've just been using them more for fun than for deep learning. It was time to give my consciousness a shock. It was time for a plant so strong, so powerful, that I would be scared, humbled, and fully reconnect myself with the immense force of Nature.

What would the medicine present to me? How would I change? Would it show me all my fears, all my flaws, or even tell me that everything I've done was bullshit? I knew many

Chapter 1 - Set and setting

people are afraid of psychedelics because they don't want to face their own darkness. I was scared too. I liked my life, I liked the way I thought, and I was proud of the things I've done. What would happen when I realise that my entire path in life was a mere lie?

But you see, that was why I wanted to do the ceremony – to check on myself, and to see if I was going in the right direction. Whatever that was coming to me, I had a feeling that I would emerge a better human being, even if it meant giving up a lot of old habits, mindsets that I believed in, and ways of doing things that I was comfortable with. Change is scary, but I was kind of ready to just go for it and see what happens.

I glanced at Olga and she gave me a reassuring nod, as if she could smell my worries. She had been through the same ceremony before, a few times, and it had helped her grow into the amazing human being she was. I was the psychedelic Rainbow Warrior, but I knew that none of my previous experiences would be as intense as this one. No acid, no shrooms, no ketamine, could prepare me for this. This was a whole new realm, the next level of my own evolution, and I knew that it was going to be fucking intense.

I was never a fan of such medicinal ceremonies, not that I've been to any before. But I've always had the impression that the other spiritual seekers would be rather irritating with their

Chapter 1 – Set and setting

self-righteousness, holier-than-thou egos, and non-stop quoting from Osho's speeches and shit. Or maybe I was just scared of embracing this side of myself, I was afraid of appearing like a cheesy hippie to others, and to myself. I was fearful of becoming the super spiritual guy who has a sanskrit tattoo that says, "Samsara" or some mantra straight out from a Krishna Das song.

Or maybe I was just too attached to my ego, I loved my physical self too much, and it had been proven that many others loved it too. So any big change to it would make me unrecognisable to my old self, or to my friends and lovers. And then I would turn into a spiritual hermit who lives alone in a cave, only to have darkness and my past to keep me company.

But today, I say, "Fuck it" to all these fears and embrace whatever this ceremony would turn me into.

Just as I made this resolution in my heart, the doorbell rang.

– CHAPTER 2 –
THE SHAMAN

Chapter 2 – The Shaman

When we mention the word "Shaman", what's the first image that comes to your mind? I bet he's got long, dark hair, slightly wrinkled golden brown skin, deep, soulful eyes, a feather somewhere in his hair, and some really traditional looking Amazonic tribal tattoo. He's even got no shoes right?

See? Preconceived notions from watching too many Youtube videos, Hollywood movies, and Netflix documentaries.

The thing is, "Shaman" has also become an overused term that has been misappropriated by white men with dreadlocks that have been to one Ayahuasca ceremony and now suddenly think that their calling is to heal the world through giving *Kambo*, Cacao, and *Rapé* ceremonies at Psytrance festivals.

There is evidence to suggest that the original term came from the ancient Tungusic Evenki language in North Asia.[2] Its original meaning is, "someone who is regarded as having access to, and influence in, the world of spirits, who typically enters into a trance state during a ritual, and practices divination and healing."[3]

---

[2] Juha Janhunen, Siberian shamanistic terminology, Suomalais-ugrilaisen Seuran toimituksia/ Memoires de la Société finno-ougrienne, 1986, 194: 97-98

[3] Singh, Manvir (2017). "The cultural evolution of shamanism". *Behavioral and Brain Sciences.* 41: e66: 1-61.

Chapter 2 - The Shaman

So even though the Amazonian tribes have been practicing their own form of healing, performing rituals, and communicating with their spirits for thousands of years, none of them have ever used the term "Shaman" to describe themselves.

So let's start again, when we think of the term "Shaman", what's the first image that comes to mind?

You see, when I opened the door, I was dumbfounded to see a very regular looking guy in his late fifties, dressed in comfortable fitting jeans and a large T-shirt walk in through the door. He had a full head of shoulder-length dark greyish hair, wore a pair of glasses with a silver frame, and looked a little bit like a hairy bear with a bit of a beard and a pot belly. He could've been your uncle who lives in Spain, running his cute little vineyard, here for a weekend visit with his daughter.

I was disappointed. My cultural appropriation was looking for someone who looked more "authentic". You know, I was hoping he would arrive at the door on the back of a giant falcon, accompanied by his three-headed serpent who also served as his walking stick.

A firm handshake like a normal human being later, he introduced himself as Moshe. Ok, well, at least the name sounded kind of exotic.

Chapter 2 - The Shaman

He didn't exactly have the mysterious vibe I was going for, rather, he seemed way too normal with his Samsung smartphone and constant Facebook scrolling. He talked about everyday stuff like who got pregnant and who else got married and all. Yes, there was a certain sense of calm and cool composition about him, but if I didn't already know who he was, I would never have assumed that he was a Shaman.

In my head, I was already judging him for spending more time on Facebook than me. I remember thinking to myself, "You've been on so many intense psychedelic journeys and you haven't found Facebook scrolling a menace to human societies? Are you not wise? Aren't you supposed to be the one teaching us life lessons throughout the ceremony today?"

Well, as you can also probably tell, all my psychedelic exploration did not as well make me a saint. I was bitching to myself in my head, scrutinising his every move, every word, every breath, for his "Shamanic Level".

Oh, he said "Shit", that's very non-Shamanic. Look at him blow his nose with non-organic tissue paper, point deduction right there.

I obviously had a lot to learn. But hey, it was my first time coming face to face with a real deal medicine man, and given my past encounters with random hippies with dreadlocks who

Chapter 2 - The Shaman

took too much ketamine calling themselves White Magicians, and Indian men with long hair disguising themselves as holy men and luring young white tourists into bed, I was on top of my judging game.

So I was having fun in my brain being a little asshole, trying not to show any signs of my negativity, when Moshe turned to us and said, "I really don't like being called a Shaman, it's an overly misused term which has now evolved to become something negative. I'm really just a simple guy who has studied decades with the wise medicine men of the South American rainforests, practiced with them for years."

"And now I bring these medicines, and their message of connection with Nature, to see how I can help people around the world. So don't call me a Shaman or don't think I'm special. Just call me Moshe."

Boom. I'm such a shit person.

- CHAPTER 3 -
THE CEREMONY

Chapter 3 - The Ceremony

I snapped out of my judgemental diva mode and allowed myself to let go, relax, and follow Moshe's instructions as we started preparing for the ceremony. My memory of the exact stuff that went on during the ceremony is a little hazy as it happened over a year ago. And really, I was just going with the flow with no intention of keeping a record, or writing a book about the experience.

It was already dark outside and we dimmed the lights, as Moshe lit up a big candle in the middle of the room, where we sat around like excited kids around a campfire waiting to hear our camp leader tell us a story.

Olga, her boyfriend George, another dear friend of ours Hanna, and me, were the four participants of the evening. It felt more like an intimate gathering instead of a big commercial Ayahuasca healing session sponsored by Pfizer or Budweiser.

In the air was the sweet, cleansing fragrance of smoking sage Moshe had just lit above the candle. He stood up, with the sage in one hand, a huge condor's feather in the other (which he produced out of nowhere), and began fanning the smoke towards each of us. As he came close to our faces, he started singing what sounded like an ancient ceremonial song in a language I couldn't recognise.

Chapter 3 – The Ceremony

I, too, began to calm my mind and clear it out from any thoughts, releasing myself from the stresses accumulated in everyday life, and letting go of all distractions.

The cleansing process continued with the introduction of rapé (pronounced ha-peh, mind you) to our bodies and minds. Rapé is a traditional blend of sacred tobacco, leaves, seeds, bark, and plants, carefully mixed and prepared through a labour intensive process into a fine powdered form.

Rapé is said to help realign the chakras, clear up negative energy, and ground the user. Personally, I'm not a huge fan of it because of the sharp sting I get at the back of my nose when it's blown into my nostrils. But since this was happening at a proper ceremony, I allowed myself to be fully open for the experience, just so I can reap the full benefits of the entire process.

As Moshe chanted something sincerely and blew the snuff tobacco into my nose, I felt a strong sensation of prickly heat shoot straight up to the back of my brain. It burned a little and my eyes began to tear at the same time my nose started running. It felt like a burst of silence and clarity to the cacophony of my busy brain, like a gush of cold spring water to my head on a hot summer day. I wiped off my tears and snot, and felt an instant state of calm.

Chapter 3 - The Ceremony

It felt extremely intimate to have someone blowing stuff into my nose, no matter what it was. At this moment, I fully trusted Moshe, but if it was someone I didn't know, I wouldn't want them exhaling their leftovers from lunch into my lungs.

The ceremony continued with more traditional songs, the partaking of sacred tobacco in the form of a cigar, more rapé, drumming, and the setting of intentions.

My intention was rather simple, but then again, could be a hard to achieve one. But hey, it's ok to set an intention without expectations right? So I looked up into the high heavens and took a deep breath, word by word, I sent this thought into the belly of the universe "Please allow me to humble myself and receive truth. No trippy visions of entities, no sacred geometry to entertain myself with, just brutal, hard hitting truth, wherever it may take me. Even if I become someone else, so be it."

I didn't intend it to be a session of enjoyment, I mean, if I was gonna enjoy it, then fuck yea. But I wanted it to shake me down to my very core and humble me.

Moshe proceeded to describe what we could expect from the session, "The medicine is going to be strong, but never too strong than what you want, and what you need. Whatever experience you have, or answers that you are looking for, ask

Chapter 3 – The Ceremony

the medicine with respect, and it will reveal to you what you need to be shown."

He continued, "You will start seeing a lot of bright colours, many patterns, or mandalas. You could choose to stay in this zone, enjoy the euphoria, relax and let it take you away. But how deep you want to go is up to you. If you want to go deeper, you just need to ask."

"Everything you see here are very old artefacts that my teacher, and my teacher's teachers, have been using for generations. They have been using it to communicate with the spirits of the jungles, their ancestors, and other powers. You might not really believe that this big condor feather does much, or this stone, or even this elaborate headgear that I'm wearing. But all these sacred objects have accumulated the energy of all who have used it, and their deep intentions of learning, and if you allow yourself to be open to it, this energy can be passed on to you."

That's the thing isn't it? I've never really allowed myself to be open to stuff. You know, objects, and the power they might contain. Perhaps this was something I really needed to learn as well.

I've always been telling others, and myself, that everything is energy, and energy can be transferred from one person to

Chapter 3 - The Ceremony

another, between objects, or from objects to people. But I've never really opened myself up to it. I get the concept, I believe it, but to feel outside energy affecting me was never really my gift.

Today, however, this might change. Everything might change.

– CHAPTER 4 –
THE MEDICINE

Chapter 4 - The Medicine

"So, if you don't have any questions, let's begin."

Moshe started to grind the Yopo seeds on an ancient looking piece of wood, just like how we would cut up the cocaine on the bathroom seat cover, but with a lot more reverence, and none of that playfulness or dodgy vibes. As he continued the grinding, he sang soulful chants that I didn't understand, but felt.

As the seeds slowly became powder, my heart started to race. This was going to be the trip of my life, what was I going to find out? Where was the universe going to take me? My palms started sweating and my breathing started to become faster.

"It's understandable that you're feeling nervous. But don't worry, you are going to be very safe. Any time you want the session to stop, all you need to do is open your eyes, let me know, and I can help bring you out of the experience."

At this point though, I was still a little sceptical of the sacredness of everything. And I almost already knew that this was to become a big part of my experience during my Yopo session. I was scared that I might get kicked in the cosmic ass for doubting the sanctity of everything, or for talking shit about religions in the past, or being disrespectful to people who believed in stuff I thought was ridiculous.

Chapter 4 – The Medicine

I always took a certain false sense of pride in my scepticism and thought that my unbelieving self was a sign that I was a down-to-earth, clear-headed smartass that refused to buy into any kind of bullshit. Maybe I was just scared of being ridiculed.

What if I get this major revelation and become a Flat Earther? How would I continue to live my life? I would never take a boat again. And I would become one of those Flat Earth fanatics they interview on TV, "Look around you, we are all around the globe."

I stopped imagining myself appearing on TV with a tinfoil hat and looked up at Moshe as he finished preparing the Yopo into four neat piles of different sizes. One for Olga, one for George, one for Hanna, and finally, one for me.

In my stupid mind, I was secretly thinking, "I hope he's gonna give me a big one. He must think that an experienced psychonaut like me can handle a powerful hit. Bring it on. Make it snow."

I was an idiot. But in this book, I'd like to be completely honest about the things I feel and think, so that you could also see that I'm a flawed, judgmental human being, just doing my best to be a good person, but often falling short of my own expectations of myself (just like all of us).

Chapter 4 - The Medicine

Olga went first. She went up to Moshe, knelt on the ground, lowered her head, and through a bird bone tube, inhaled the brown, earthy powder into her nose. In a few long, gentle inhalations, she finished her dosage and went back to her seat on the couch.

We were advised to sit on a chair or couch with our feet on the ground, our elbows on our knees, allowing our heads to drop with our hands holding our foreheads. In front of each of us, in between our feet, was a huge bucket just in case we needed to throw up (it's quite common to throw up in such ceremonies because our bodies can sometimes feel the need to purge the toxins that the medicines are clearing out).

George was next, then Hanna with a smaller pile of powder, then it was my turn.

I walked slowly towards Moshe, knelt down, and took the reasonable sized pile of woody, herby smelling powder up my nostrils. It didn't sting nor irritate my nose, it felt very natural and even healthy, just as medicine was supposed to feel.

I felt no immediate effect. But now that it's in my system, we'll just have to wait and see what happens. I returned to my seat, put my forehead on my palms, looked down at what seemed like a black hole of a bucket, and waited.

Chapter 4 – The Medicine

Moshe started singing sacred songs about Yopo and fanned the smoke of burning sage onto us. The sweet fragrance filled our consciousness as I tried to clear my mind of the "wait".

You know, the first times you take any kind of substance, you always go like, "When is it gonna come? How is it gonna come?" Yea, I was like that too. But slowly and surely, I was sucked into the melodic voice of Moshe, letting it create swirls of colours in my mind's eye, and hearing his song warp into a "wao wao" kind of twisty psychedelic sound.

– CHAPTER 5 –
THE BLUEPRINT OF THE UNIVERSE

Chapter 5 – The blueprint of the universe

I forgot how long it was that I tripped on the now pulsating music and the shamanic drumming. But when I realised that the medicine was taking its effect, I could already not hear anything except for a low pitched buzzing in my brain, and with my eyes closed, I could see vividly the ever changing multicoloured mandala in my pineal gland.

It glowed so bright and shone with so many different colours that I could almost perceive a completely new colour that has never before existed. Call it whatever you want, it's a new colour.

The mandala pulsated and bloomed upon itself like an eternal flower, resembling the tanka art of Tibetan monks, combined with the flower of life and all its sacred geometry, changing its colours with every breath I took, and transforming its composition with the sound waves of my heartbeat.

I didn't particularly feel any sense of euphoria or heart opening sensation like psychedelics sometimes give. But rather, it was a dense, heavy feeling, as if the seed was carrying an atomic load so huge that it weighed down on my head. And this morphing mandala was just an entrance sign, inviting me to finally take a step into eternity.

I had seen this before, a few years ago in Goa, when I passed out on the dance floor after smoking Lucid Tulsi. What I

Chapter 5 - The blueprint of the universe

understood during that time was that I was invited to observe the blueprint of the universe – the sacred, geometric perfection that all of existence has been created according to. I didn't see that as an entrance though, the colour show was all I was invited to. There was no door to walk through. But during that time, it was already perfect, it was the ultimate bliss.

I learnt never to question who created that blueprint, or why. Simply because that was like asking to see God's face. Audacious.

It was the final door of psychedelics that I've never been able to pass through. I thought those who did either went insane, killed themselves, or started some weird end-of-days cult. Or I was under the impression the knowledge was never meant for us i.e. humans did not need that knowledge to survive, or even live happily ever after on this planet.

To see that blueprint taught me that all of creation was sacred, and based on a simple, beautiful formula that resonated with the vibration of ॐ Aum (it's a four-syllable word representing the past, present, and future, and the last syllable, silence, stands for all that is unknown). And that little glimpse of reality was more than enough to open my mind and soul up to eternal love, compassion, and kindness.

Chapter 5 – The blueprint of the universe

Or that was what I thought.

Today, I saw that there was a next level I could walk into. I guess finally going through that door would be fucking nerve wrecking. Who would I come face to face with? Whoever, whatever, the omniscient, omnipotent, and omnipresent god, the giant spaghetti monster, or some super advanced alien being that owned my soul?

Would I get there today? What would be revealed?

I acknowledged the sacred blueprint and asked the Yopo, "Ok, I've seen this before, and I'm ready to go on to the next level. Take me all the way, break me out from all illusions and give me the hardcore truth. I am ready, I am humbled, and I accept whatever may come."

Once that request was submitted into hyperspace, a reply came back immediately into my consciousness. I couldn't tell what kind of answer it was, because it started something like this:

The entire mandala started vibrating and the low pitched humming picked up in its volume and frequency. The vibration got more and more violent and it felt like my entire existence was shaking to its very core. The ringing in my ears tuned its pitch higher and higher, and it got louder and louder.

Chapter 5 - The blueprint of the universe

It came to a point when I thought the shaking was so intense I was going to pass out and the screaming buzz in my ear was so deafening I was going to explode.

What was happening? Waaaaaaaaaaaaaaaaahhhhh…

Just when I thought everything was going to go "Boom", just like a spaceship finally breaking out of the earth's atmosphere and is suddenly flung into the vacuum of space, everything stopped.

Darkness. And silence.

– CHAPTER 6 –
WHY ARE YOU SPEAKING IN MY VOICE?

Chapter 6 - Why are you speaking in my voice?

What? Where am I? Why is nothing happening?

I dwelled in the darkness for a while, ready to embrace what was going to happen next. And then, from the abyss, came a voice that sounded exactly like mine (well, at least what I think I sounded like in my head).

"So, what do you want to know?"

Wait, what? Who are you? Why are you speaking in my voice?

"I am the Universe. So of course…"

The voice came with a facial expression of "You don't really need me to complete the sentence, do you?" It's kinda a combination of "Come on, you're a little smarter than this to figure it out" and "Don't ask stupid questions you already know the answer to".

Well, everything happened in the dark. There was no face, but rather, a feeling of that facial expression deep inside my guts. It kept the tone of my own voice, but a lot more reassuring, kinder, and nicer.

Of course, if the Universe spoke to me, it would use the one single voice I most related to – my own.

Chapter 6 – Why are you speaking in my voice?

"Right, hello Universe?"

"First question, go."

Oh, no pressure here Mr. Universe. I meet god in a dark alley of the milky way of my soul, what the fuck do I ask?

I was in a little bit of a panic. Where do you even start? Reincarnation? Past life? The future? The state of humanity? Veganism?

"Look. I know you don't know what to ask. You'll get the hang of it in a while. And no, I am not reading your mind. I am you.

First of all, you're on the right path in life. Whatever direction that you are heading towards now, whatever you're doing, whatever you're planning with your writing, your travelling, your relationships, you're doing right. So don't you doubt yourself, or let anyone's judgement or opinion cast fear on you. Chill. You're good."

Wow. Even the tone is so me. Universe, great job. You really know me well. Woohoo! I think we'd have a great time hanging out.

I've always sort of had a clue that we are all manifestations of the universe. Like deep inside, our so-called souls are made of

Chapter 6 - Why are you speaking in my voice?

universe stuff but I'm not really sure of many things still. I mean, I've had a hunch, but I never really wanted to commit to it until I found out more.

"What were you waiting for? All the things you wanted to believe about the Universe is right. You just didn't dare to go for it. You were afraid of being ridiculed. You were afraid of making a commitment to this truth because it was easier for you to linger on the edge of 'look at me I know something, I'm smart, but I'm not stupid enough to say that this is true because what if it's not'."

Ooo, harsh.

"Look. Fear no more. Here comes the truth. It's not a matter of believe anymore. It just is."

– CHAPTER 7 –
YOU'RE FINE

Chapter 7 - You're fine

"For a long time now, you've been afraid. I know your biggest fear is that one day you get some grand realisation and find out that your whole belief system based on peace, love, unity, respect, and freedom, is just bullshit. You're just saying these things without truly believing in them. And that you've gotten so used to saying these things, getting so much positive feedback, that you just keep saying it.

You're afraid that one day, someone will come up to you and burst your bubble. Your whole hippie life, your whole philosophy of love, will then come crashing down and you'll be left with nothing."

Fuck me. Yes. Exactly.

"This fear was there because you didn't truly allow yourself to commit to the truth. You were still searching for an even more convincing truth. When you stand on the edge of belief and just hang around the fence, you're bound to fall because you had no firm ground to stand on. You wanted to meet god and stare it in the face before you believed in the divine. Here you go Kai, this is what you've been waiting for. Fear no more."

My dearest readers, for those of you who have known me over the years, or read my last book, you would've understood that I am generally, a very commitment phobic person. I never truly had a strong opinion on something because I always

Chapter 7 – You're fine

believed that maybe a better, stronger, more powerful argument would come along, and then I'll just adopt the new belief and keep growing.

I thought that was a rather healthy way to do this whole "life" thing. What I believed in was only what I believed in temporarily, and I stuck to it until something else better comes along.

But that also meant I didn't really know anything.

"Kai. Stop doubting so much. All you wanted to believe in is real. Free yourself from the shackles of doubt. One more second you doubt is one more second you live in fear. All these judgment of others simply comes from a fear that they would judge you. Free yourself from this. You don't need to carry this burden. There is nothing to believe. It all just is.

Your first book was a good effort. But you could also see how hard you judged others. It's a good starting point for you, and yes, it still serves as a good guide for many people, and a good voice for the psychedelic tribe. But you have grown, and the second book shall be written with the truth that you will choose to embrace."

This was how I decided that I had to write this book, to tell you in pure honesty about the evening I met the Universe.

– CHAPTER 8 –
WHY DO WE EXIST?

Chapter 8 - Why do we exist?

Ah ha, the million dollar question. Of course it is the first question that popped up in my mind. For the longest time, humanity's prophets and philosophers and religious leaders have all been trying to crack this question. And so far, we've gotten answers like "God created us because He loves us", or the atheistic "We're just a random bunch of particles that collided and caused the Big Bang, and billions of years of evolution later, we're here."

I kinda felt that we've never really gotten a satisfactory answer. And I really wanted one. So I asked.

"You've met me before, do you remember? A few years ago in Goa? I showed you the entrance but you never walked through. Simply because it wasn't your time yet, and you didn't even know that it was an entrance you could walk into.

During that time, you felt infinite bliss, infinite joy, and infinite peace, didn't you? That was you staring at my face, or the blueprint of the matter Universe, the mandala, the Aum , the emptiness of everything, and the fullness of nothing.

At some point, you got bored because nothing was happening. In your own words – no life, no animals, no friendship, no romance, no trees, no oceans, no music, no art. The nothingness had everything in there, but still, it was nothing.

Chapter 8 - Why do we exist?

And when you got bored, you came out from the trip and all you desired was once again returned to your existence."

Yes, that time, when I decided to come out from the state of bliss, I actually saw myself (in my head), coming out of a womb and being reborn into the arms of all my friends.

"What you felt was what I felt. I wanted experience, I wanted an infinite unique number of ways to experience myself. That's why I manifested myself into all the galaxies, all the milky ways, all the life, all the aliens, all the beings in all of existence. For an experience."

So there are aliens?

"Of course there are aliens. There's a whole bunch of them you can't even detect with your five senses. You could be staring at one right now and you wouldn't even know it's there. There's definitely stuff that you can also see and hear, but whether they are trying to make contact with humans is up to them."

What do you mean up to them? Aren't you the Universe. Aren't you them, too?

"Yes, yes. But I manifested everything with their own free will. I had a blueprint I put into place. The blueprint gave birth to all the planets and the multiverses you can see and not see,

Chapter 8 - Why do we exist?

and those you didn't even know existed. Why the blueprint? So there's a stable, perfect formula for everything to work in such a way that allows life and non-life to flourish, evolve, and spawn, creating even more unique experiences for me. I can't have planets exploding all the time into nothingness again right?

So for me to have infinite unique experiences of myself, I also had to put some limits on how much I was inside the heads of each and every one of you. In essence, I am you, but the limits I've put for myself is to be a mere observer in your lives. Simply because if I was also thinking for you, everyone would think the same and we would all have the same experiences, same conclusions, same opinions. You see how that's hardly an interesting experiment.

And the limits I've put on you humans? Your brain that is smart enough to know that you are me and I am you and we are all one, but not smart enough to once again become me. If not we'll all go back to the same old single, common experience of life. Again, kinda boring.

That's why every animal, every human, every grain of sand, every snowflake, is unique. Sure, you wouldn't be able to tell a grain of sand from another, even with your most advanced technology. But the experience of each sand grain is different. They're on a different position on the beach, no matter how

Chapter 8 – Why do we exist?

minute that difference is. They move in their own way with every wave and tumble around to a completely new position.

I've made every moment a unique experience for me. In this very split second, while you are sitting here listening to this word, a child is picking up a rock on his way to school in a rural village in China, a red car with the number plate QZ 4523 is driving past the main square in Gothenburg, oh, and a leaf just fell from a particular tree in Gambia.

The combination of all these events all across the universe at this very instant, is unique. They have never happened before, and chances are, they will never happen again. Every moment is special, and when you truly learn to appreciate the Now, you will celebrate every single breath of your existence. That's a pretty good way to live. And to indulge in the riches of every moment, is why everything exists, and it is never boring."

– CHAPTER 9 –
IS THE UNIVERSE LOVE?

Chapter 9 - Is the universe love?

Right, so everything is just an experience. Nothing more, yet, nothing less. What about love?

Here's something that might be a little controversial for some of us. We've always seen inspirational quotes and heard from gurus and wise spiritual people that the core of the Universe is love.

We've believed that the Universe has a plan for us, and that it loves us, and everything is just love. I honestly never really quite understood that. There are planets that rain glass shards sideways, where's the love in that?

"The Universe just is, Kai. I am only as old as you are, as curious as a toddler, and as playful as your neighbour's kitten. I am all of you.

In the animal kingdom, predators hunt and kill their prey all the time, sometimes for food, sometimes for sport. There is no love there, or at least the human kind of love. If I can eat you and keep myself from being hungry, I would. But such is the natural balance of this planet. It has been set in motion by the perfect blueprint – it's a total balance, a seamless cycle.

In this world, there is fighting, there is bloodshed, there is pain. But do I love all these experiences? I cannot speak this way. I just am. Deep within everything, but yet, somehow just

Chapter 9 - Is the universe love?

a detached observer. Love is part of the blueprint of this planet so that adults will take care of their young and humans will get along with one another. Love is present in every facet of your life so that you will fully enjoy and cherish your experience, just like I completely treasure every unique experience of myself through every single one of you.

I am not love. I just am what I am. I am. Love is built into every human experience, every animal experience, even every plant, so that you will see life as worth celebrating and living. Many humans would say it's the greatest force in the world, yes, and to feel loved makes you want to continue living. Love is here for all of you to see the value of life, so that I may continue experiencing myself through your life."

Why then, when I first went into the deep trance, or my first heavy trip where I saw all that sacred geometry stuff, did I feel so loved, so much warmth, and so much bliss?

"Love is the peak of your human experience. Infinite joy, infinite love, infinite safety. That's to show you how great the human experience is. That was the purpose of your trip then. You were meant to catch a glimpse of that, and then come back and live life to the fullest, and to help as many other beings as you can do the same.

Chapter 9 - Is the universe love?

Compare that to this experience now. It's dark, it's empty, it's nothingness. That's because you've broken through, temporarily, mind you, the human experience. And this space is also pretty conducive for a conversation. Now you are feeling what the universe is feeling. Nothing. It just is.

I created you to experience your human dramas, your highest joys, your deepest lows, your greatness, your fear, your lust, your potential. All of it, I can only experience through you.

Now do you see how much all of you mean to me? You are my unique experience. Every human, every plant, every burst of life, every rock in the ocean, every drop of water. You can choose to call it sacred, but that's not a word I would use. Everything just is, no more, no less."

– CHAPTER 10 –
WHY DO WE DESIRE ENLIGHTENMENT?

Chapter 10 – Why do we desire enlightenment?

Wait, so if every one of our mortal lives is an experience, why is everyone in such a hurry to "lose their egos" and get to this stage where we call "enlightenment"?

"Your brain, your consciousness, your body, this whole thing is also what you've always called the ego. There is nothing wrong with identifying with it, really. Again, if everyone identified themselves as the universe and thought what I thought, we'll all be the same being – not so fun.

Of course, there are many different interpretations of what you would like to call enlightenment. In your brain Kai, you're probably clueless. You think that unity with the one consciousness, one eternal soul, also known as the universe, is enlightenment. Let me tell you, everyone is guaranteed that. Yes, when you die. The white light at the end of the tunnel comes back to me.

You lose all of your ego, your personality, your sense of self. And taadaa (not sure if the Universe actually used this word, but I wanted to add it in for dramatic effect), you are me and I am you, without your physical being.

What you have always misinterpreted as enlightenment, Kai, is actually a temporary union with me, catching a glimpse of the Universe, then coming back to fully live your human life. Simple as that.

Chapter 10 - Why do we desire enlightenment?

So in fact, you are enlightened, according to this definition, but hey, that doesn't make you a saint, nor does it make you less of an asshole sometimes.

==Being enlightened simply makes you responsible for spreading the message of how to live life to the fullest.==

You don't become special after enlightenment. You just have a new mission. You could call it a burden. But hey, really, what else you gonna do?

But also, don't take your mission so seriously. The 9–5 office worker, what you hippies always call "slave to the corporate world" or "Babylonian", is also my unique experience. As long as they're having fun, experiencing love, enjoying their own lives, it's all good.

==Your job is just to help open up their minds to what could possibly be a nicer way to treat themselves.== It's not that I need that from you. It's simply because many people could learn to enjoy their lives a little more, and that's where you come in, or everyone who has met me.

This whole misinterpretation of enlightenment as a permanent state of bliss after you die, free from the cycle of reincarnation, is again, a very human kind of desire. It somehow ignores the fact that all of existence has been put into being because the

Chapter 10 - Why do we desire enlightenment?

Universe desires to experience itself. When the Universe, the collective consciousness, or us, still wants to experience itself in matter form, we will always have more reincarnations. There will always be more puppies, more trees, more planets, more aliens. Because we all want to.

Enlightenment isn't a solo mission. We are all one soul, one consciousness, one being. When together, as one, we decide to be enlightened and not exist on this plane anymore, we will just return back to nothingness, the ultimate zen, the Aum . Nothing happens anymore. We just are. That's our enlightenment, collectively.

Nothing would have existed in the first place if I wanted to stay in this state of being, Kai. Nothing. Not even the blueprint, or any of that sacred geometry stuff. No bliss, no joy, no feelings, just zilch. This whole reincarnation thing is my constant desire to continue experiencing myself in newer, more unique ways. Respect that.

And about reincarnation, it is all of us collectively deciding what to become next. If you've been a bully this life, when you die, then maybe together, we'll decide that for a learning experience, we'll manifest our energy into becoming someone who will always get bullied in the next reincarnation.

Chapter 10 - Why do we desire enlightenment?

Do you now see that saying that you are the child of the Universe, and then go on to say that you no longer want to be reincarnated, doesn't quite fit together so well as concepts?

Don't be in a hurry to become nothing. We've only existed in matter form for a few billion years, we're just getting started here. There's still a lot to look forward to.

– CHAPTER 11 –
DO YOU BELIEVE IN KARMA?

Chapter 11 - Do you believe in karma?

Karma's a bitch, or so they say. I've never quite understood the concept of karma properly. And I can safely say that many people don't really understand the Buddhist concept in all its complexity, or simplicity.

I thought karma was simply, "I do something bad, something bad will come back to me in some way or another. And if I do a lot of bad in my life, I will be reincarnated as a cockroach. The opposite happens if you do good, you might be reincarnated as Curb Kobain, start a band called Samsara, but you get to live a happy life until 72."

Karma was always an individual thing. Like we're all single souls trying to reach enlightenment and finally escape the endless cycle of reincarnation and life on earth as a creature to be always subjected to pain.

I've also been told horrible stories of the 18 levels of hell when I was a kid. There even was a section of a Chinese Fable theme park in Singapore dedicated to scaring kids into unquestioning obedience. If you've been a liar in your life, you will have your tongue scalded by boiling oil in level 9 of Hades, and then have it devoured by ferocious ants.

So Karma worked well as a good scare tactic for a big part of my life. But the desire to do good somehow came from the desire to gain something back for myself, whether it's a nicer

Chapter 11 - Do you believe in karma?

reincarnated form, or a more short-term, winning the lottery after I've donated a dollar to the Cancer Foundation.

So when the concept that the whole universe is One came into my consciousness, my misconstrued idea of karma didn't seem to sit too well with it. It seemed too self centred to fit nicely into the "we are One" point of view.

So of course, this was also a burning question I had to ask when I got the chance to.

"Ah, yes. Karma. Your guess is half correct. ==Individual karma does exist.== Put simply, when you do something good, like for example, share your food with someone, you put out good energy into the world. And at some point or another, when you put out enough good energy, you start surrounding yourself with people who appreciate this and are eager to give back to you.

When you do something ==bad== though, the ==karma== that comes back to you is usually ==more immediate.== It comes in the form of guilt, regret, and paranoia. When your mind gets filled with all these negative thoughts, everything that happens to you, even if they're only minute obstacles, you start attributing it back to the bad deed that you've committed, and you start feeling like nothing is going your way. Of course, in the longer run, this might create in you some sort of "since nothing is going

Chapter 11 - Do you believe in karma?

smooth for me anyway, I might as well continue down this path of destruction, what could go worse" attitude.

So that's individual karma. But to look at the bigger picture, we indeed, go back to the fact that we are One. Whatever energy you choose to send into the Universe during your existence will stay in the Universe. A singe selfish act of yours can trigger a butterfly effect and eventually snowball into a catastrophe. Well, even if you do something with the best of your intentions, someone else's bad energy might come into the chain of events and still result in some catastrophe. So what you do definitely matters, but what we all do together matters more.

Your soul is not singular. There is only one soul in the universe and that is all of us. The same goes for karma and reincarnation. You can do all sorts of bad things and live a tortured life, but at the end of the day when you die, you leave this reincarnation and once again become one with the Universe. The Buddhists might have a different point of view, but the so-called enlightenment after death is guaranteed.

So then, as one consciousness, one mind, one soul, we decide what's our next experience. If many beings have led miserable lives during their reincarnation, we might together decide to go for "the good life" in our next manifestation.

Chapter 11 - Do you believe in karma?

Of course, it's not as simple as this. Time is not linear. Your current reincarnation is only, say, 80 years on average. And humans have existed for under 200,000 years. When you compare this number with infinity, this is a mere split second. So what you humans say about past lives and next lives, to me, it's all happening in an instant. But that's something you don't have to try to figure out because this information is useless to you. Your ego is modelled to deal with time in a linear sense. So, don't try to overreach.

But then again, what you do as an individual does matter when we're talking about our next reincarnation. But what everyone decides collectively, as one mind, is what really sets the wheels of Samsara in motion to begin your 'next life'."

At this point, I somehow felt that when the Universe said the words, "Next Life", it said them in inverted commas. I didn't exactly see the Universe do the two-finger action with both hands, but I experienced it with all my existence.

"Oh, and allow me to let you in on a secret. No one has escaped the reincarnation cycle as an individual. Yes. For one to be enlightened, the One has to be enlightened. All of the Universe."

Chapter 11 – Do you believe in karma?

Ah, so maybe that's why the Buddhists are this eager to spread their philosophy to all of humanity. To get all of us enlightened, together. Super noble cause.

"So again, the so-called enlightened one is the one who understands this, and comes back to help others see the point."

– CHAPTER 12 –
DID THE RELIGIONS GET IT RIGHT?

Chapter 12 - Did the religions get it right?

Much of what I understood about religion is a very worldly, follow-the-rules, "believe in this guy and gain eternal life" point of view.

I personally believe though, that all the major religions are talking about the same thing, just that they originated from different prophets, across different eras and different cultures.

Everyone talks about love, kindness, compassion (well, I don't know what happened with the whole Noah's Ark and the crusades and all that madness). All of them offer some kind of promise, whether it's enlightenment or a place in heaven, and almost all of them have some sort of rules.

"Right, religions. You see, the truth has been explained to you quite simply so far. And really, that's about it. The prophets have all gotten this same message and tried their best to communicate it to people. Mohammad, Jesus, Buddha – they were all amazing human beings doing their best to help humankind.

Some of what they've said might sound outdated, or even barbaric to you, but they made perfect sense for the people during the times when they walked the planet. It was all about love and being nice.

Chapter 12 - Did the religions get it right?

Of course Jesus was the son of God, I mean, I wouldn't put it in these terms, but it was easier for people to relate to. He saw that he was a manifestation of the Universe and that everyone was also an expression of the Universe. Maybe he didn't have the best communication skills and vocabulary, but everything he said was right, and said with the best intentions.

And the same goes for the other great prophets. People during that time just didn't listen, or they didn't understand. So a bunch of men interpreted the message in their own way, wrote some holy books, and made up their own religions to get as many followers as possible, for whatever reasons they came up with.

Did he die on the cross to save humans from sin? No, he didn't. He got put on the cross because some people didn't like his message. And he didn't really die and get resurrected. They couldn't find him in the cave because some of his followers rescued him and helped him escape somewhere. Of course they kept it a secret, they figured that letting anyone else know that he was alive would once again land him back in captivity, more torture, and real death.

Oh, and why did these prophets receive the big message? No, I didn't appear to them in dreams or some divine intervention. It was through meditation, and psychedelic plants and fungi."

Chapter 12 - Did the religions get it right?

It didn't occur to me to ask who was high, and who gained their knowledge through meditation. During this journey, it just didn't quite matter to me so much. Or maybe I was already so overwhelmed by this information that I simply forgot to.

I know that what I've written above is considered a complete heresy to many readers who are religious. I really want to clarify that these do not represent my personal opinion and I am merely recounting the conversation I had during that ceremony. You could look at it like I just made everything in my head up because I was under the influence. But I'm just a lowly messenger, writing everything I experienced here, in as much detail and clarity as I can remember.

I am being as honest as I have ever been, and I know that I will be judged by many for this. But hey, I'm just a regular guy trying my best to do good.

"So why does humankind receive these messages about the Universe and life? ==It's always freely available to help you live life and appreciate every single moment better.== It's as simple as that. Nothing more divine, nothing more complicated.

So, why haven't more great prophets appeared, you might ask. Well, they're all over the place. They are all of you – musicians, writers, spiritual teachers, artists, even engineers. The masses

Chapter 12 - Did the religions get it right?

just spread love and compassion through different mediums, but the message has always been the same. That, my friend, is what had been prophesied as Jesus' second coming.

But this time, instead of making one guy bear all the responsibility, this message has spread to numerous beautiful human beings so that humanity doesn't once again, make a religion out of it and make the same mistakes of separating yourselves from one another, and from other species.

You see, that's why spirituality is the new thing that's catching on. It's a mix of everything humans used to understand as religion. You don't brand yourselves any longer as Christian, Hindu, Zoroastrian, or whatever. You're just a spiritual being.

So yes, you're a messenger, just like Jesus, Buddha, and a million other people. Nothing so special. ==This spirituality is built in your blueprint, the very same blueprint I used to build all other planets, suns, stars, and the blackholes.==

You'll of course, remember this experience in an imperfect manner, reinterpreted and reimagined based on your own ego. But be as honest as you can, and write without fear. Be glad you have found your medium to transmit the message. You're on a good path."

CHAPTER 13
THE EMPTINESS AND FULLNESS OF THE EGO

Chapter 13 – The emptiness and fullness of the ego

Now after that whole "I am a messenger" topic, my ego has been all inflated into a multicoloured balloon of my own greatness.

"Calm yourself. It is perfectly fine to enjoy the greatness of your ego, you were hardwired to enjoy it. But please, don't get carried away and think that it is you.

You wouldn't call your hand you, just as you wouldn't say that your beating heart is you. The same goes for your current thought. Or ideas. They just pop into your consciousness sometimes. Would you say these define you? Your mind is, as well, not you, it really is a beautiful system of particles, energy, and electricity that helps you store and process information.

But what's really you? You already know. You said it on your slightly pseudo-intellectual Facebook profile yourself, that you can't describe yourself without getting the Universe involved.

What's really you, is me, is everyone on this planet, everything in this Universe, and everything that has ever existed, and will exist in all planes of existence, for all of time. The Beatles actually got it right when they sang "I am the Walrus".

But your ego then, is just a tool to help you navigate your surroundings and to help you survive and experience life. You don't have to take it seriously at all. Yes, there's stuff you can't

Chapter 13 – The emptiness and fullness of the ego

really change, such as where you were born, who your parents are, and all the stuff that you've experienced in the past.

But that, too, doesn't at all define who you are. It shouldn't even affect your current self. The material sense of self can be redefined at any moment.

==If you want to be known as a good person, just decide, and then be that, right from this point on==. That's how empty the ego can be. Of course, the blueprint has set certain limitations for every species so that you can be a unique permutation of greatness and flaws. So if you're born with a slightly different makeup, for example, if you were born blind, you can't possibly just decide to see. Or if you were born with a certain kind of brain that makes it difficult for you to function in modern day society, you might also not quite be able to change your own brain chemistry to fit in perfectly. That is your unique experience. My unique experience.

Yet, ==your blueprint, how your entire body functions== (stuff you learn in biology), the entire evolution of life of earth, has brought your human physical form to what it is. How your neurons fire when a thought arrives in your head, how your instincts tell you to avoid pain, how everything in your body functions so perfectly. ==That is the fullness of your ego.==″

Chapter 13 - The emptiness and fullness of the ego

I found myself starting to cry. Uncontrollable tears that just flowed from being invited to perceive and understand the divine beauty of everything. Everything seemed perfect as it is. The entire Universe is perfect. There is no good, nor bad. It just is. Just an experience.

I felt freedom. I didn't need to live up to any social expectations. I didn't need to live up to the name of Kai, my parents' hopes of me one day becoming a great author and make loads of money. I didn't even need to live up to my ideal of myself in being a good writer, or pressure myself into being the best person I could be everyday.

I am nothing. And yet, I am everything. I am free from the constraints that I have allowed society, my heritage, my social circles, my education, and my own mental shackles, have set on me.

I heaved a big sigh of relief, and wept. And as I did, I felt the Universe embrace me in my entire presence. Incredibly safe, deeply warming, and greatly comforting.

I allowed myself to be cradled in this moment for a little while more, soaking the love in and all that.

– CHAPTER 14 –
SO EVERYTHING IS PERFECT, INCLUDING TRUMP?

Chapter 14 - So everything is perfect, including Trump?

Wait a minute. So if everything is just an experience of the Universe, why all the evil? Why Trump? Why the obsession with money? Like, how does that fit into the whole love and compassion and all the messengers here to do the good work to make life on Earth better?

"Look, Kai, there really is no good and bad. The whole "love" thing was built into your blueprint just so that you would continue loving your own life, and you would want to continue living through your ego, and really enjoy it. The potential for universal love is within you.

But not everyone sees love the same way. Humans all have some kind of definition of their own. And yes, even though pure love is selfless, without conditions, without expectations, given freely to all of life, not everyone agrees – due to their own upbringing, cultural norms, expectations, and many more factors.

Some people love power, some people love to exploit others, some people love to inflict pain, others love to receive it. Humans define love differently. And yes, it is all part of the experience – the experience of the Universe, through your flaws, your failures, your anguish, your conflicts, your torture, your senseless violence even.

Chapter 14 – So everything is perfect, including Trump?

Am I cruel? Maybe to you, because life on Earth and being a human is your only role here. But to me, everything just is. You were built with a certain level of free will, and it's up to you to exercise it. ==My role here is a mere observer. I do not interfere.==

Just like you when you meditate. You're just trying to get closer to how the Universe actually thinks. A thought passes, you observe it, but you don't dwell on it, you don't interfere with it. You passively watch it come into your consciousness, not identify yourself as the thought, or with it, and then watch it drift away.

This is what it is when I'm observing humanity."

My self righteousness was getting bruised badly. All this preaching about doing good for other humans. All that, "You alone can't change the world, but if you could make one person's day just a little better, it's all worth it." What for?

"You feel the need for justification for your good deeds, whether they're small acts of kindness or huge noble causes. That's because you still see yourself as a saviour of some sort , you need to be perceived as being a good person – your ego needs to be pampered and stroked.

Chapter 14 - So everything is perfect, including Trump?

This way, you still see life as an individual. Of course, it's only natural that you do. But all of life itself is a learning process. When all of existence, mind you, not just the sentient beings, is one, everything you see as "bad" is just something to learn from.

Say, you like to dwell on Trump when you talk about evil. Well, it's true that this guy with a ridiculous haircut and seemingly low intelligence is wrecking havoc here on planet Earth. He's part of the great cosmic joke, also a unique experience for humanity to learn what's it like to have a democratically "elected" leader that is not capable of bringing peace to this planet. It's for humanity to learn about the inability of current political systems, or any political system, to contain, or control the power of the human spirit.

Many people and animals are suffering in the process, but this could ultimately serve as an awakening for all of humanity. An awakening that could one day, be looked back upon as the single, most powerful event that saved you from extinction.

When you look at all worldly events as a big picture, through the lenses of the Universe, everything becomes a lot more significant, or less important, depending on which point of view you take. There isn't duality here in my realm, everything just is.

Chapter 14 - So everything is perfect, including Trump?

Yes, there's definitely a certain level of suffering here on this planet. Pain has been built into your blueprint so that you could learn to avoid it. Being hit by someone else is painful, so you'll learn not to hit others or avoid being hit. Being lied to by someone is painful, so you'll learn not to lie. Being bullied or emotionally abused is painful, so that you'll learn not to inflict that on others.

It's all here to help you learn to be honest, compassionate, loving creatures living as one with the entire planet. Animals feel pain when attacked by predators, so they may learn to run away and try to survive, to cherish their lives. That is in the blueprint.

It is free will that takes pain, and abuses it as a weapon. And humans seem to be doing this a lot.

Could I have created the Universe with less pain? Yes of course, there are billions of Universes in existence without pain, and billions with more pain. You're not the centre of existence. You're just one of the infinite solar systems that are happening right now, and it just happens that your world is one that is created with pain, and the avoidance of it, as an encouragement for continued life and harmony.

You might feel that it's unfair. You might feel that you have been lied to when they told you that God was benevolent.

Chapter 14 - So everything is perfect, including Trump?

Well, in a way. God, or the Universe, or you, isn't all benevolent. For your world to function seamlessly as it is today, pain has to exist.

Maybe one day, your planet might evolve into one with no pain. That's not up to me. I've set the blueprint for all earthly creatures to have the capacity to understand oneness and move on to a kinder, more compassionate existence. The rest is up to you guys.

So you see now, it's all perfect?

That doesn't mean you could just ignore it all and refuse to do anything about it though. Like you told your readers, if you can make one being's day just a little bit better, or eliminate some of their pain, why not? It makes you feel better too, yes?"

I suddenly felt the need to throw up. Knowing that the bucket was securely tucked in between my feet, I allowed myself to hurl whatever I had to get our of my system into the bucket.

Nothing physical came out though. I puked, but no fluids, just sounds. Perhaps whatever I was expelling was in energy form? At this point, anything could be possible. I smiled, took a deep breath, and continued the journey.

- CHAPTER 15 -
IS THERE HOPE FOR HUMANITY?
ARE WE WAKING UP?

Chapter 15 - Is there hope for humanity? Are we waking up?

Personally, I've always been at two minds about this question. On one hand, it feels like more and more of us are "waking up" to the destructive ways of our highly industrialised way of living. And many of us are switching to a vegan diet, fighting against the injustice against other humans and species, reducing waste, taking up sustainable farming and living. It feels like we're indeed moving towards a more aware humanity, and finally taking our survival seriously.

Or at least that's what it looks like on my Facebook feed, which is based on a "Kai is a hippie and likes news about veganism, sustainability, and good news about legalisation and stuff" algorithm.

On the other hand, humans are still producing insane amounts of waste, far right groups are gaining more and more political power, and oil companies are still drilling into the heart of Pachamama.

If we look at the entire planet Earth as a single ecosystem (it is), and one living, breathing organism (yes, it is), humans are now seen as a virus that is threatening the health of the planet. Are we then, going to be wiped out like a disease? Will there be more powerful cancers, influenzas, disasters caused by global warming to decimate our population? Or are we going to "wake up" quickly enough to realise that we are indeed part

81

Chapter 15 – Is there hope for humanity? Are we waking up?

of the delicate balance in the ecosystem and live in harmony with it?

How hard do we have to push the message of sustainability so that we can all be allowed to continue living on Earth? Make no mistake of self-righteousness here, we are not doing all these to save the planet.

Sure, we're pushing a lot of creatures to extinction as we trample along our destructive path, and there's always something we could do about it to help pandas make more babies, or we could also adopt more black rhinos. But when humans finally go extinct because we've made this planet inhabitable for ourselves, Earth will still be around doing Earth stuff. Life will continue to flourish, and weird creatures of all forms will emerge.

Earth wasn't fashioned just for humans, we evolved to thrive according to the conditions of this planet. When we go, nobody will miss us. So tell me, Universe, are we fucked?

"We can't be sure, really. That's something that's out of my control. We are all One, and for humans to continue to survive, you have to start acting like you're actually One and collectively, turn the desire to survive into sustainable action.

Chapter 15 - Is there hope for humanity? Are we waking up?

The will to live and procreate is in your blueprint, and so is your connectedness with all the other creatures, plants, and life on this planet. You see, it's all supposed to work seamlessly when the whole planet is behaving as a single organism – not with a single mind, but as a single body.

Dinosaurs came and went. Ah, those were fun times. It was all nice and dandy with giant cockroaches and everything, until the meteor came. Boom. And then we repopulated Earth. So are you going to perish as well? You can certainly try not to. It would be nice for all of you to realise the beauty of existence, the complexity of human emotions, all the drama that's uniquely human, and make yourselves work according to the laws of this planet.

You might ask, why are humans the only creatures on this planet that are destroying our only home? It was all good when we were all living as hunters and gatherers. We lived off the land and took only what we needed. Then we had agriculture and industrialisation and we've landed ourselves in this state.

All the other beings on Earth seem to understand that we are One. Why not humans?

Well, there really is no answer to this question. What happened, happened. It just is. You are not any more special

Chapter 15 – Is there hope for humanity? Are we waking up?

than any other manifestation of the Universe. Some beings evolved to thrive, some beings evolved to perish. Before humans existed, many different plants and animals have also come and gone. If it works, it works. If it doesn't, then bye bye.

There wasn't a special plan or anything. Everything just unfolded on its own free will. And that's the excitement of life. If there was a grand plan, or a chartered course, the whole experience would be bland and predictable. I would never be able to surprise myself.

Imagine watching a movie where you already know the whole plot. Yes. Why bother? So back to the question of whether humans are waking up – you are. And there's hope. That's why so many of you are fighting the good fight. All the hippie farmers, the sustainable communities, the green movement, the solar power technologies, we are heading towards survival. Real survival that is one with the planet. Not the kind of short-term survival based on selfishness.

So many of you already have important roles to play – artists, writers, shamans, activists, celebrities… You're getting it right. Keep going. We can't say whether humans will definitely survive, but while we're still here, we can make life nicer and simpler for other beings. So go ahead, be strong, be kind, and do that.

– CHAPTER 16 –
WHAT ABOUT THE NEW AGE STUFF?

Chapter 16 - What about the new age stuff?

I've always been sceptical of millenials branding themselves as "light workers" on Instagram and using this newfound identity to navigate music festivals and yoga retreats.

So the first time I tried crystal healing, I wasn't expecting myself to feel anything. It was at Ozora Festival a few years back when I decided that I should really try it for myself instead of rejecting the whole concept of healing.

So this guy was doing it for free throughout the entire festival, booked full of appointments everyday. I went up to him to find out more and maybe write something about him for the festival newspaper – Ozorian Prophet.

"Look, I'm on my lunch break now, and I don't have any more slots for a full healing session, I'm all booked up until the end of the festival. But hey, I'd give you a quick one. Hold on to these two pieces of granite."

Ok, so just like that? These two black palm sized rocks could do something special for me? I held them in my hands and closed my eyes, while I stood there beside him and tried to clear my mind of any thoughts or distractions, or judgement.

Within a couple of minutes, I felt as if tree roots were growing out of my feet, extending themselves into the ground, rooting me firmly like I was a giant tree. It was super weird. These

Chapter 16 – What about the new age stuff?

roots reached deeper and deeper down, absorbing whatever nourishment the ground could provide. I felt my body and soul somehow neutralising itself, and Mother Earth herself was recharging my energy.

"Now slowly open your eyes. Did you feel very grounded?"

No fucking way. How did he know how I felt? I told him what went on in my mind and body, and he explained, "Yes, granite has strong grounding properties that reconnects you with the energy of the earth and keeps you rooted."

I was baffled. I've always had friends giving me crystals and telling me what they could do, but this time was special. I actually felt something physical and real. And from that point on, I learned to respect the art of healing, but only when performed by real masters who had undergone proper training and intense studying.

It really isn't the art of healing itself that I'm sceptical of, it is the #influencers who sound all airy fairy that I'm doubting.

So Universe, what can you tell me about all these?

"Everything is made of particles and all particles contain energy. Even this is new age sounding to you, I know. But all

Chapter 16 – What about the new age stuff?

==particles vibrate at a certain frequency that affects other particles that come close to it.==

It isn't rocket science. Before the Big Bang, everything was only energy. There was no matter, just energy. It is this energy that spins the planets and rotates the universes. This energy, naturally, is in everything that has been created.

So every object, crystals, artefacts used for ceremonies, or even a metal spoon, can receive energy from people or other objects, and can also pass on energy to them.

It is only natural that crystals can be used to alter the energetic properties of your body and make you feel better. Of course, that is, if they are properly charged and the people that are performing these sessions know what they're doing and which crystals to give you.

Remember the giant condor feather that your shaman used for this ceremony? It does indeed contain the intentions and energy of the previous shamans who have been using it for decades. So it is important to treat it with reverence and not contaminate it with bad intentions.

The same goes for many places of worship and pilgrimage sites. These are not exactly special places, nor are the images of Jesus or Mary or the Buddha actually magical. You'll notice

Chapter 16 - What about the new age stuff?

that you always feel a sense of peace, calmness, and hope when you come to these places. That's because they are so strongly charged with the energy of pious worshippers' respect, hopes, and dreams. When they come to these places, they bring all their best intentions and honesty, that they actually affect the overall energy of the place permanently.

Now that you already know that everything is just as sacred as everything else, you can also learn to respect the people who find certain objects or places extra holy. You might not feel that a church is any holier than the forest, but to them, it holds a special position in their hearts and minds, and you can learn to respect that.

It isn't about the place or the object itself, but rather, the people who truly believe that these are sacred. Allow them to feel what they feel, and respect their beliefs.

You might find the condor's feather a ridiculous thing to carry around. But to the Shaman, this is important stuff, and today, you learn to respect what people hold true in their own realities.

Of course, like we discussed before, everything has its own energy field. And if you truly open yourself to feel this energy, even the sceptical you can feel something special.

Chapter 16 - What about the new age stuff?

So once again, stop being so uptight. Let go of your fear of being spiritual or new age. There is power in the crystals, truth in the Reiki healing, wisdom in the artefacts. Trust."

CHAPTER 17
THE SHAMAN DOESN'T READ HOROSCOPES

Chapter 17 – The shaman doesn't read horoscopes

When Moshe first walked into the apartment earlier that day, he looked disappointingly normal. He was constantly checking his Facebook and chatting with random people on Messenger, took part in a little gossip session, and was even showing us cat videos on his phone.

I kept thinking that he didn't feel, or behave, very "shamanically". I kinda expected him to exude a more holy vibe, or speak slower, or constantly spitting out words of wisdom.

"A Shaman is like a doctor. He knows his medicines well, how they work on different people, and has decades of experience doing this.

A doctor, like all other humans, have their own paths in life, their own flaws, and their own personal issues. You had preconceived notions of what a Shaman might be and how he should behave. And when he turned out to be someone different from your as-seen-on-TV impression of him, you were naturally disappointed.

Moshe is here to be your doctor for tonight. He is here to share his knowledge in his field, and to provide you with this experience, which could've turned out disastrous if he didn't give you the right dose, explain everything clearly to you, and

Chapter 17 – The shaman doesn't read horoscopes

hold the ceremony accordingly. You have him to thank for this conversation.

He is to be respected for what he does, not what you expected him to. There are many things he understands much better than you do, and some things that you know better than him.

He is not here to bring you the message of truth. That is your job as a messenger. He is here to give you the medicine and perform the ceremony so that you could have the optimal learning experience.

Whether he's addicted to Facebook or gossips about other people does not change the fact that he is a doctor. It doesn't reflect how good he is at his role either. He isn't Jesus, nor Buddha, both of whom have their own set of flaws too.

He isn't here to tell you about your own spirituality either. That's our job, and that's what we're doing right now.

Just like yourself, you write your books and articles in the most honest way you can. But you also tell your readers not to judge you too harshly for not living up to the philosophies you've tried to explain in your writing.

Chapter 17 – The shaman doesn't read horoscopes

We're all trying to be the best people we can be. And Moshe's doing an amazing job at being a shaman. He isn't a guru, so don't put these unrealistic standards on him.

And even if someone's bad at their jobs, it isn't your job to judge them. But instead, see where you can help out, if you, indeed, know better.

It could also be the case where someone's doing something they're not at all good at, and maybe their talents could be found, and used somewhere else. Humans judge one another so harshly, and most of the times, it's done to make themselves feel better. Don't fall into this trap of needing to put down someone to elevate yourself, you are already perfect as you are, just like all of the Universe. Just be kind and help one another along."

– CHAPTER 18 –
THE HIGHEST FORM OF SPIRITUALITY

Chapter 18 – The highest form of spirituality

Self-proclaimed spiritual people sometimes piss me off. There's always this holier-than-thou attitude as they glide around in their long robes looking like Jesus or Mother Mary.

And they've got these eyes when they look at you, those that give you an impression of wisdom and ultimate kindness. You know, it's kinda like the half open eyes you do when you're looking into the sunset on the beach and feeling the bliss of life. That look creeps me out.

Oh, and the way they lay their hands on you softly with a reassuring touch? It always feels like they're trying to tell you, "Don't worry my ignorant child, trust my divine wisdom, everything will be alright." Condescending.

This has come to a point where telling someone you're spiritual just sounds super pretentious, and it comes with hashtags too.

"Remember that ==your kindness is the way towards a nicer humanity reflects== directly on your own spiritual development. You can't expect others to listen to your message when every other word you utter is that of contempt, intolerance, and a lack of compassion.

Different people have their own spiritual journeys, and for most, their paths are always paved with good intentions.

Chapter 18 - The highest form of spirituality

However, when taking the first baby steps, it could be easier for many to follow what seems like a more superficial approach. For example, joining a yoga and meditation class at the local gym, diving into buying crystals, hippie clothes, and sacred geometry jewellery, reposting inspirational quotes from popular teachers such as Osho, going head first into horoscopes, astrology, energy healing... You know, all the stuff that you always laugh about.

But that's at least a good start. ==Be happy for everyone who has started on their own spiritual development.== It is you who always said that even though our approaches are different, the destination is the same – greater compassion, happiness, and love.

Instead of throwing snide remarks at your fellow human beings, humble yourself and gently give guidance to the beginners, and let go of your fear and scepticism, and learn from those who have something to teach you.

All the stuff you call new age are actually ancient sciences and wisdom. Despite being popularised on the Internet today, much of what is shared are still very relevant today.

It is your own fear of being ridiculed, or being wrong, that makes you lash out against these spiritual practices. Let go of this fear and learn what you can. What's the harm of knowing

Chapter 18 – The highest form of spirituality

a little more about crystals? What's the danger in understanding more about the planets and how they affect our everyday lives? The more you know, the more you can use the knowledge to help others.

You thought your scepticism and sarcasm was funny. Indeed it could be. But you could also be very rude and childish, poking fun at things you haven't even bothered to find out more about. It's fine to laugh about things, but please, do it with compassion, not ignorance. Laugh with everyone, not at them. Your own actions say more about your spirituality than theirs.

The highest form of spirituality is service and kindness. Now that you've had this conversation with the Universe, your path forward is to share what you've learnt selflessly, use this knowledge to serve selflessly, and help others understand that this wisdom did not come from you, but from all of us.

Help others who are not so knowledgeable, equip them with little pointers here and there. And regarding those who are on the same path as you, see where you can serve them in terms of your writing, and all that you have gained. Remember that everyone is your guru. You might be able to offer guidance, but everyone can teach you something valuable that you didn't even know you didn't know.

Chapter 18 - The highest form of spirituality

Treat every being, including all plants and animals, as your teacher, and respect them as you would your parents.
Sure, you will be rewarded with just enough material wealth. But once you're on a path of service, understand that you will never be financially rich, because when you have more, you will want to give.

Free yourself from the shackles of judgement and love freely. Only when you bow your head, humble your soul, can you allow yourself to be truly blessed and serve everyone.

Since we are all one, when you serve, you will also receive. The joy of serving and humility is all yours to enjoy. And don't be afraid to receive. For when you bravely receive, you allow another a chance to give.

Once again, enlightenment isn't disappearing back into oneness, or hiding in a cave to meditate for decades. Enlightenment leads back to service. Remember not to create a following around your ego, let everyone understand that you are no one special and that everything that you know, we already do. You are a mere channel, our combined consciousness is the source, so don't make the mistake of all the false prophets and fake gurus. Remember you are nobody, and everybody."

– CHAPTER 19 –
MANIFESTING STUFF

Chapter 19 - Manifesting stuff

It seems quite popular these days for people to use the term "manifesting". From what I understand, this usually means setting our intentions, sending it out into the universe, and hoping that the universe delivers it to us.

This seems to suggest that when we're on the right path, or the path that the Universe agrees on, then whatever we desire would somehow be delivered by the Universe on a silver platter.

There exists a multitude of Youtube guided meditation videos that claim to help us "manifest love", or "manifest wealth". I find it difficult to believe that they even work, because we don't always get what we want, even if it's with the best of intentions.

"Kai, you see, manifestation is misleading term that is widely used in vain. When you want something, you set your intentions, go out there and be on the lookout for opportunities to bring you closer to your goals, bravely take those chances, fail a few times, continue working hard, very hard, and see where it all takes you.

You might not get what you want in the end. There are no promises that the Universe can give you, except that you're fine.

Chapter 19 – Manifesting stuff

When you have expectations, you're taking an infinite number of possible outcomes from your endeavours, disregarding the fact that every one of them has an equal chance of happening, and demanding that all the conditions be set perfectly to point you only towards that single result that you want to see.

One out of an infinite number of possibilities? You're definitely going to get disappointed.

As a single, collective, all knowing, all seeing, all encompassing intelligence, we do not have the ability to manifest the future, or expect any outcome.

What we can do though, is to create love, contentment, and appreciation in ourselves regardless of outcomes. Sure, humans can always desire and try to work towards what they want. But the key to happiness, and in this case, true manifestation, is to be contented with whatever result that may be presented to you.

When the Christians preach, "God might not always give you what you want, but always what you need," it is not to say that the Universe knows what kind of future situation would be right for you, but rather, teaching us to take whatever that comes with gratitude, and seeing everything as a lesson.

Chapter 19 – Manifesting stuff

Then, we'll see everything that happens as a gift from god. The manifestation of goodness comes from the inside. When you take things positively, everything becomes a good enough result. When you desire happiness, you manifest happiness from within, and whatever happens on the outside will be looked upon with joy. When you desire love, you become love with the whole of your being, and whatever you encounter would be a loving relationship."

CHAPTER 20
WAKING UP TO A LIFE OF SERVICE

Chapter 20 - Waking up to a life of service

"Do you have anything else you would like to know?"

At this point, all that information was already a lot to process. Of course, there were loads more I would like to understand and learn. But for the time being, I was overwhelmed, tired, but invigorated with life at the same time.

I wasn't sure what more I could ask. I'm quite certain though, there would be questions in your mind I have left unanswered. I had no idea how much time had passed, it was irrelevant.

All the questions that bugged me in my life had just been answered with a clarity that my own brain, my psychedelic experiences, or anyone I've read, could never deliver. Of course, I might not be so well read, and I'm sure many readers already knew, long ago, all the things that I've shared in this book.

I had no doubt that I had just conversed with the Universe. It was so wise, so impartial, so compassionate, so harsh, yet, so me.

It was comforting to know that the Universe was only as curious, as young, as playful, as wise, as powerless, as we are. Yes, because we are the Universe, together, and when I was speaking to it, I was also speaking to you.

Chapter 20 – Waking up to a life of service

Some would say that it was just a DMT entity that I spoke with. I suppose that could also be true. I haven't met any beings in my psychedelic experiences who spoke to me before in such simple, clear, non-cryptic terms. And it would be kinda shit if the entity lied to me about being the Universe.

For those of you who've had more experiences with Ayahuasca and breakthrough DMT trips, please feel free to share with me what you think about my conversation, and if you've had similar encounters.

"If you've got no more questions, do you want to see something fun? Open your eyes."

It was the first time in these few hours that I allowed myself to open my eyes. And even though I knew that we all had a bucket in between our feet, just in case we needed to throw up, it was gone, and replaced by a black vortex that opened up straight into nothingness. What the fuck?

This was too much. I mean, not too much, but it was just so sudden it took me completely by surprise. I let my eyelids sink and once again heard the voice of the Universe, this time with a cheeky, tongue-in-cheek tone, "Fun, right?"

I smiled. The Universal sense of humour. It just made a cosmic joke. Haha.

Chapter 20 – Waking up to a life of service

"I think you're ready, Kai. Everything you needed to know about living a fruitful life, being a good human being, and what to do from this point on, you have learnt in this conversation.

There's a lot more stuff about everything – all the science, all the non-linear time, all the black holes and more – that you wouldn't need to know to do your job well.

Humans don't need to know so much about space and time and our origins to understand what life is about. All you needed to do was to be honest with yourselves, look within, and appreciate the present moment.

And when you truly live the now to the fullest, you already see the meaning of life.

This is the most important message you can spread. Not just through writing, but through how you live everyday, every moment. You don't even have to preach too much, just the exuberance of life could inspire others to also indulge in the present.

But if you choose to write this book, write it with all honesty, stay humble, and never ever claim these ideas as your own. It belongs to all of us. You, me, every single particle in existence, throughout all of time, we are one."

Chapter 20 – Waking up to a life of service

Printed in Poland
by Amazon Fulfillment
Poland Sp. z o.o., Wrocław